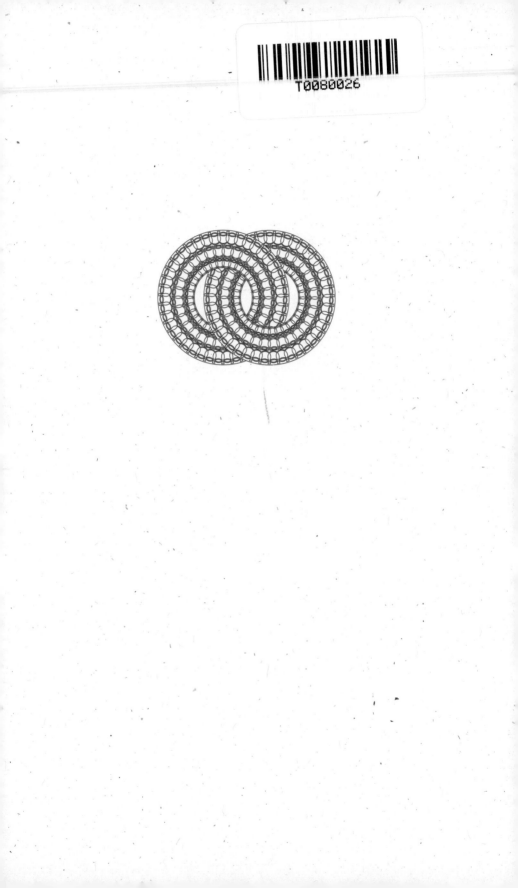

MISERY ISLANDS

MISERY ISLANDS

JANUARY GILL O'NEIL

CavanKerry ❖ Press LTD.

CavanKerry Press Ltd.
Fort Lee, New Jersey
www.cavankerrypress.org

Publisher's Cataloging-in-Publication
(Provided by Quality Books, Inc.)

O'Neil, January Gill, 1969-
[Poems. Selections]
Misery Islands / January Gill O'Neil. -- First edition.
pages cm. -- (Emerging voices)
Poems.
ISBN 978-1-933880-46-4

I. Title. II. Series: Emerging voices series.

PS3615.N435A6 2014   811'.6
QBI14-1554

Cover photograph used courtesy of the author
Cover and interior text design by Gregory Smith
First Edition 2014, Printed in the United States of America

CavanKerry Press is dedicated to springboarding the careers of previously unpublished, early, and mid-career poets by bringing to print two to three Emerging Voices annually. Manuscripts are selected from open submission; Cavankerry Press does not conduct competitions.

CavanKerry Press is grateful for the support it receives from the New Jersey State Council on the Arts.

ALSO BY JANUARY GILL O'NEIL

Underlife (2009)

CONTENTS

THE GOSPEL OF LOW ART

IN THE COMPANY OF WOMEN

MISERY

TETHER

To Alex and Ella, my silver linings

We all have reasons
for moving.
I move
to keep things whole.

—Mark Strand

come celebrate
with me that everyday
something has tried to kill me
and has failed.

—Lucille Clifton

MISERY ISLANDS

THE GOSPEL OF LOW ART

I am terra firma by way of airship,
by way of mist and fog to clear blue easy.

I'm in transit; don't know what state I'm in,
by way of upgrade, by way of centigrade.

I'm flying over the inner cities of America,
over brick and click, over dirt and trail,
over cardboard, glass, plastic, and tin.

I am hope by way of heart.
I am conjoined twins named Progress and Excess.

I am the trees that fall in the forest
but everyone denies hearing.

I am a nation in foreclosure.

I am every cigarette butt and pull tab
left by the side of the road.

I am pawn shops and payday easy-loan shops,
my sidewalks are paved with scratched lottery tickets.

I am everyone named Lucky and Chance.

I am every child who won't come home tonight.

Every three minutes, someone kills two birds
with one stone. The crime is never reported.

I am Killington, by way of Stone Mountain,
by way of Death Valley.

I am every sex shop and tittie bar
named Golden Banana and XXX.

I am every mill town and boarded-up factory,
the assembly line disassembled, the layoffs,
layaways, and laid to rest.

I put the depressed in depression.
I am America reconstructed; I am a force at work.

I dig a ditch, I fill a ditch.
My collar is white, my collar is blue.

I am the missing 23 cents out of every dollar
a woman is supposed to earn
but doesn't.

I am every God damn it and Lord have mercy.

I am America by way of Africa,
Mexico, Ireland, Poland, and India.

Land that I love,
I fly over you,
look down at you,
dream my American dreams about you.

Every second of every day,
I am cardboard
I am glass
I am plastic
I am tin.

A stout man enters the vestibule of the bank.
Afternoon light splits itself into a half light
as he fumbles for the bank card in his wallet.
He's tired, and smells faintly stale.
Maybe he just got off work, needs a few bucks
for gas or beer or for tonight's dinner,
pork chops and potatoes,
a meal his wife will surely cook
as soon as he walks through the door.
His fingers tap the ATM keys. Then
there is this unexpected song,
a mouthful of air gathering
into a chorus of *No, No, No, No, No, No, No*
in sync with the machine's rhythmic beeping.
He pauses; listens to his own breath come and go
as he tries to catch it, his funds insufficient,
the question of capital asked and answered—
the money is somewhere yet nowhere.
It takes him a moment to remember where he is
and that he is not alone. He pulls out his cell phone
to have that uncomfortable conversation
about not having enough, about what to do next.
There is squawking on the other end of his smart phone.
He hangs up, searches his pockets for his keys, excuses,
a plan B, as the machine spits out a receipt like a tongue
     sticking out
from its tiny sliver of a mouth. While here in this chamber
the lungs dispense a heavy sigh. And for this
you don't have the words.

But you are the pens, the paper,
the report due yesterday
with its charts and figures.
You're the tilting desk
that no one, not even you,
bothers to fix. Take a swig
of burnt coffee and get to it.
You fix things, you buy things,
you're a connector, a decider,
you find mistakes in statements
buried in the coal mines of words.
You are also the banter, the fodder,
the guffaw in the corner office,
the high five and the back slap.
You're the secret knowledge
that you're the only one here
who has a clue. How quickly
the hours move as you buy time.
You're a wealth of information
in an economy of scale.
Like the clock on the wall you make things tick.
Nevertheless, you are not your salary—how could you be?
You are the window overlooking
the golf course and the Q-tipped golfers
hitting balls into oblivion.

His days are spent hunched on bad knees
cleaning durable microfiber, generic
rent-to-own living room sets
covered with juice stains, pen marks,
blood from a knife wound, smelling
of urine, human or otherwise.
You'd be surprised how many people
pick their noses and leave the evidence
under the arm of an armchair, he tells me.
Roaches, bed bugs, pet hair, dander—
you name it, it's there, in the fibers,
the polyester pillows and dense cushions.
Steam vapor removes almost anything,
even tar from a chaise owned by a guy
who works at an asphalt company,
working his ass off in 10-hour shifts
to afford his slice of America.
What lies beneath is a mutiny
of forgotten cheese curls, Cracker Jacks,
paper clips, socks, hot dogs, barrettes,
crayons, condoms, needles.
He is a priest keeping secrets
for the sex worker's love seat,
or the sectional repossessed
the day before Thanksgiving.
They think it's theirs but know
otherwise and treat it as such,
without permanence. Still,
it will be re-rented to fit someone else's
wide bottom or skinny hips
just like new, gently used.

And this work that makes
the back crack and muscles ache,
this salvation in salvage
is a dirty job that someone has to do.

They stood in line with me,
listened intently to conversations
around us, the giggles and whispers,
stifling their joy as they have for years,
decades, centuries—the absentee voters.
And when we entered the voting booth,
I heard their weeping. Their hands on mine
darken the circle on the paper ballot,
our grip on the pencil tight enough to break,
the weight of us overflowing.

At 16,
I worked the concession stand at Circle 6 Theatres,
offering butter flavoring on large tubs of popcorn
and upsizing large drinks to the size of vats.
I envied the folks who entered those dark rooms
and came out changed.
The shopping mall where the theater was located
was a Petri dish of human interaction—
young Navy boys on shore leave
trying to pick up high school girls
looking to cement their jailbait status
with their jailbait friends.
After the late-night movies ended,
I'd walk down the house aisles to find everything
from used condoms to drink cups filled with chaw.
I hated it all, the front lobby hookups and breakups,
the unflushed toilets and syrup-covered floors.
When I came home from my evening shift
I smelled like burnt popcorn, my feet sore
with the overworked-underpaid burn that comes from taking it,
a burn deeper than flesh or muscle should bear.
I stayed at the job through most of my high-school years.
Wasn't until later when I moved away from home
that I tried all those things the lobby kids did in darkened theaters.
Now, Circle 6 is closed. The mall once filled with destinations
is home to stores with cool yet misspelled names:
DRESS 4 LESS, VIZIONS, KOOL SHADES.
Rarely do I smell popcorn and not think about
the hard work of making people happy.

That big nipple of a dome where my father
took me to see pro wrestling matches—
I remember the blue cotton candy he bought,
the glossy program we used to spot
"the villains" from "the good guys."
The giant ring was an 8-foot cage
that barely contained the likes of Andre the Giant,
"Nature Boy" Ric Flair, Hulk Hogan,
"Rowdy" Roddy Piper, Ricky Steamboat,
and Jimmy "Superfly" Snuka.
Who knew it wasn't real? Anybody could see
there was something inside that
hurt so much it wanted it out.

It was a swirl of violence
with a few thousand strangers
shouting out their sad aggressions.
"Kill 'em!" "Beat 'em down!" We yelled
from our safe distances while they honored us
with body slams and clotheslines.
We were enthralled. The mock ballet of body blows
and pile drivers, grown men beating each other
until purple splotches blossomed from their eyes
and blood gushed from nose to mouth. Two go in,
one comes out. It is matter of fact, swift and gory.
We took it all as truth, as the gospel of low art.

Shake your fingers,
let your tree trunk arms
dangle below your belt.
Under the surface,
a river of lava begins to seethe.
This is who you are.
Feel the muscles unfurl
above your forehead.
Let go of the voices
calling for your annihilation.
The grimace around your mouth
gives away too much in this moment,
which is all that matters. Runners at the corners?
You've got this. If the catcher throws signs at you,
throw them right back. Give 'em
the split-seam, high heat all the way.
A double steal is in play—don't get rattled,
you're made of pure will. Start the play
around the horn: one-six-three—
double play! The runner will argue the call.
Benches clear, but it's over before it begins.
End of inning. Your job is done. You are a stop gap.
Another one-and-done for the books.
Remember, this is where you live.

THE HAWK AND THE HARE

—for JK

When the world you know shuts down for the day,
turns off its halogen lights, uncrumples itself
from the missed foul shots around the recycle bin,
you cape your jacket around your neck
and leave the office, only to be startled by
a red-tailed hawk a few feet away,
light brown feathers streaked in white.
He stands on the newly sodded lawn,
magnificent, suspicious, wings tucked in,
yet does not let go of what's between his talons:
a chipmunk/no a squirrel/no a hare—
that same small creature you saw at lunchtime
with its soft, floppy ears scampering along
the building wall, obscured by the big-headed hydrangeas.
He buries its beak into the body ripping brown fur
and skin in large bloody chunks.
He must have plotted this destruction all day
and will not be denied by you or your presence.
No sound but the sound of struggle, while your heart
pounds the insides of your body. You think, for a moment,
you should do something/call someone/stop this,
but you don't. You keep this carnage to yourself,
the hawk now grasping it tightly but inching away from you.
You're not even sure if the hare is still alive
but for the twitching of its foot, rhythmic as a drum
until it ceases. Before you know it, the hawk takes off
clasping what's left of its meal, giving a shrill cry
as he soars above the pines and disappears.
For days, tufts of hair and bone dot the grass
untouched like a makeshift memorial, as if

you could claim this handiwork as your own. And you,
the whole time, are left thinking about this savage life,
how it takes from the body and never gives back,
how it pulls you apart each day and goes on
without apology/or warning/or end.

IN THE COMPANY OF WOMEN

The body knows it is part of a whole, its parts believed
to be in good working order. It knows it's getting older,
years ticking off like pages on a desk calendar, your doctor's
appointment circled in red. Try not to picture the body
sitting alone in the waiting room. The body creaks up
and down like a hardwood floor, you tell your doctor this;
he says your breast is a snow globe. He says, *Inside there's
a snowstorm—my job is to decipher a bear from a moose
in the snow.* He flattens the breast with a low radiation
sandwich press. The body wonders if its parts will turn into
Brie cheese, if its fingers will fuse and become asparagus
stalks. He says it's possible, but don't give it a second
thought. He says insulate your body with spinach. He says
true understanding of the body will enable it to live long
and live well. But the body knows when its leg is being pulled.
The body is a container of incidental materials. If it listens
carefully, it can hear its own voice making the wrong sound.

BATHING MY MOTHER

She braces herself against the rush of hot water
and her whole body responds in relief,
the first she's had all morning.

Leaning against the shower wall we begin
the way I would if I were bathing a child—
quickly, as not to prolong this simple act.

I lather soap between my fingers,
carefully unfurl my washcloth over her skin
so as not to touch her new breast missing its nipple.

It is all business, my hands rotating in circles
down her hips and between her legs,
her body slick as a sea lion's.

She reaches around for the cloth
with slow and deliberate movements
as if not to admit pain, not to convey need—

the caregiver needing care, the care taker
not taking as she usually does. Not today.
I want to tell her I love her

but I don't. I cover her with a towel
and some small talk, try not
to notice what's missing.

No words, yet I listen
like a stethoscope
for her to say something.

Praise our scars—
the small gashes
and the long,
serpentine tracks
that make up
our unbeauty.
Scar, from the
Greek word *eschara*,
meaning place of fire.
This is the body's politic,
reminding us that
the past existed.
Inside, what is tender
is retreaded by our living,
by wounds in the sidewalks
of dry skin. Never once
do we question
the sinkholes our bodies
drive into and repair
day after day.
No one but our lover
can read the map
to our hurting.

IN THE COMPANY OF WOMEN

—for CM

Make me laugh over coffee,
make it a double, make it frothy
so it seethes in our delight.
Make my cup overflow
with your small happiness.
I want to hoot and snort and cackle and chuckle.
Let your laughter fill me like a bell.
Let me listen to your ringing and singing
as Billie Holiday croons above our heads.
Sorry, the blues are nowhere to be found.
Not tonight. Not here.
No makeup. No tears.
Only contours. Only curves.
Each sip takes back a pound,
each dry-roasted swirl takes our soul.
Can I have a refill, just one more?
Let the bitterness sink to the bottom of our lives.
Let us take this joy to go.

Don't fall in, I tell her,
as she straddles herself
over the American Standard.
I listen, we listen,
cooing and cheeping
for the pale yellow trickle
to begin between her legs.
She leans toward me, each of us
anticipating this small miracle,
the body turning energy into water,
and baby into girl-child.
The shit comes later, I think,
from those places only she can reach.
This is body's value proposition:
what goes in must come out,
changed, transformed
by this ritual connecting us all,
the acceleration of water
joining a boundless river.
It will be years before hair thick as vines
covers her trapdoor, years before
she dots her I's with a heart,
or pierces something—an ear
or lip or the soul of a boy.
There's so much to teach her
about this handwritten world.
But today, we listen for rain
through the gutter pipes.

LEGS: DESCENDING, ASCENDING

— for EDS

Because you have always been attracted to ordinary mysteries,
because you understand the exquisite language of women,
because you inherited them from your favorite aunt,
it was no surprise to see a pair of legs leaning
against your bookcase—alabaster white, fiberglass,
perfectly shaped in their stillness. No static arms
and hard breasts to complicate things, just the legs
with a metal rod jutting above the hips
like a sawed-off spine. She was the secret you carried
before you gained access into the elsewhere of girls.
In polite conversation, she became the unmade coffee table
or floor lamp you'd make one day
when no other explanation would do.
How can I not lay a hand on them,
my fingers touching those thighs,
the curve of her hip, the peak of her knees,
her open stance ski slopes of desire? Imagine her
once a model for hosiery or some other finery,
something black-laced and unmentionable
covering her mesmerizing allure—
the imagination and its strange discretions.
This nude figure, truncated, always descending
and ascending the stairs of dreams.

My aunt makes a well in the flour
with the measuring cup. She takes

the first of three eggs, cracks it
into the cup, then adds to the mix.

This is how you make a cake, one egg
at a time cracked carefully, separately,

as not to taint the whole or its parts.
In my 39 years, I have never cracked a bad egg,

never found blood in the yolk. But my aunt,
who seems to have been given a basket of them,

goes on, without explanation or pause,
adds oil, cocoa powder, mixes the ingredients

into a brown paste and shoves everything
into the hot mouth of the oven.

We let things rise the way women do
to make something near perfect,

as the egg becomes part of the whole
as the cake's edges pull away from the pan.

Still in our nightgowns, we giggled our fizzy laughter
before breakfast. Annie was a little taller than me
with stringy blond hair that fell over her shoulders,
an athlete—all the boys wanted to be her friend.
We shook popcorn out of the sheets, put away
the foldout couch from our sleepover
in my parents' den, wood-paneled
and insulated from the rest of the house.
Through her gown, I saw her breasts
small and raised, each curved like a cone and firm,
not like the flat plains of my sixth-grade chest
or the low-hanging fruit I carry now.
Hers popped like a tent and I wanted to know
what was under them, inside them: milk, water, air?
I asked if I could touch them. I placed my hand on one,
her nipple firm like a pink eraser. Then I leaned down,
put my mouth over her left breast. I remember
that first taste of skin and not knowing what to do,
whether to kiss or suck. Before I could decide,
she pulled away and I unlatched my lips.
The mere contact was enough for both of us to know
we knew nothing—we said nothing—and it was over before it began,
in that delicate girl-time before we changed and started the day.

Make peace with what cannot be seen
and what you do not know.
Try not to enter the pond scum,
the algae that swirls
in dark, empty rooms called water.
Pretend your body is a submarine—
impenetrable, even to your own thoughts.
Those breasts, underinflated flotation devices.
Your thick middle will keep you buoyant
though your arms, slender as sea grass,
won't save anyone, not even yourself.
This is a world for one: the current's
sublime lilt, the mumbles of light
from drunken stars. Nothing,
not even you, goes unnoticed.
You can swim for hours
and never get away.

The "4" is a woman with her arm
buttressing her crooked back. The "0,"
a breast, still rounded and cupped,
waiting to be touched by her husband
as he lights a candle on the nightstand.
She watches the flame sway and bend
while the light embraces the shadows.
How quiet they are, the two of them
approaching this new age. Her curves still
amaze him. The light quarters them into
equal parts radiance and desire,
the fine gradations, the parsing of glow
and gesture, how the room encloses them
in this hothouse, these forms doing nothing more
than following their functions.

AFTER MAKING LOVE, I LEAVE TO WRITE A POEM

Already I am making myself lighter,
willing myself to our quiet, unlit office
where fallen hydrangea petals litter my desk
and the rain leaks through a hole in the roof.

Here, I am most proud of my life:
the blessings of words, the way they shape
this house and the hours that move inside it.
He knows I go to answer some grim wisdom

his body has pressed into me, perhaps
the new music made by our old bodies
while night slides itself into sleep. I feel
the bliss of blue, those heavy-headed stalks

leaning closer and closer to earth. In this hour,
he is the vase in the room holding my flowers.

In a dark time
there is always chocolate.
Each bite is the perfect bite,
sweeping over the hemispheres
of the brain like a lunar eclipse.
Otherworldly in its bitter sweetness,
it awakens some hunger,
some growl in you that can't be sated—
you feed it and it feeds you.
It lingers on the tongue's tiny alcoves
leading you into some momentary depravity,
into desire and longing and sin.
No one can stop you in this place
infused with darkness,
and what you cannot explain
you accept as indulgence
long after it melts.

THE LITTLE MERMAID WALKS AWAY

There's too much water in the ocean.
Each wave an echo, an unanswered wish
calling her to the surface. The pulsing current
through coral reefs means nothing to her
when the ocean's craggy floor
is pocked with the things
others throw away. She brushes her
cyclone of tangled hair with a fork.

How perfect does an apple taste?
A steak? A kiss? At night, she writes
her girlish notions against shafts of moonlight.
The morning hands them back.
There are no flaws in nature, so to walk
on pronged feet, to leave a footprint,
means walking out of a dream.
It means destroying a kingdom
only to build it again.

The Oriental fire bellies are singing.
They are splayed under a plastic tree branch
beneath a fluorescent sun, croaking their soft song,
a clinking bell only I can hear.

I am looking at them and they look at me
as a threat, I guess. One clearly arching his back,
rising up with his slimy fat body pressed flat
against the glass, all unken reflex,

showing me his toxic orange belly and his
come-hither-and-I'll-kill-you bullshit stance.
That's cold-blooded, my friend.
You will never attract a female like that,

but I hear what you're saying.
The night is long and slippery.
We have no words to speak of
so let's not talk of dying,

or finding perfect happiness,
not tonight. We're all in this together.
Show me your true colors
and I'll show you mine.

Let's heed the call and rise
out of the trance of ourselves,
secrete our souls into the world.
We are just too young to get old.

MISERY

Even the vegetable garden has its own narrative.
Watch as I dismantle this eyesore:
a mound of dirt and rock bordered
by cinder blocks. Good intentions,
terrible execution. Nothing about it leveled
or anchored, and the netting of backyard oaks
kept the light from conversing with the basil,
with the tomatoes rotting on the vine.
Neither of us willing to give it
the hours of care to yield a harvest.
Nothing left here but the detritus
of last fall's leaves and in the far corner
a profusion of chives, green and vibrant,
enough to make me think, just for an instant,
there's something here worth saving.

It cannot save itself when it expires
like a tire's slow leak. It cannot bring back
the greediness of youth

> mouth on mouth,
> skin on skin, that gnawing,
> that longing you carried

until the next time
and then there is no next time.

You never see it coming but always see it leaving.

It waits by the door, bags packed,
full of stones from your life.

> What it can do is mark
the distance between Point A and Point B,

which feels like a galaxy,
> every star you ever wished upon
> imploding before your eyes.

JANUARY IS A MONTH YOU WOULD CONSIDER LEAVING

The days seem shorter inside me.
Everything is scorched by grief
and always there are layers.

Our conversations slow to mere breaths.
No words, just plumes of steam
vanishing into the thankless air.

I can't compete with the failing light
from your voracious heart
burning us both into nothing.

Something has left us.
Every droplet of joy evaporates
to sky. When will melt come?

How could anyone blame you
for wanting to escape
the coldest month of the year?

It was the year you displaced waves of silence
the way the body displaces water in a pool
the way the bed remains sullen from your depression.

It was the year our neighbors bought a hot tub
splashing their happiness in our faces. I watched
from the bathroom window hoping they would boil.

It was the year I knew we would never be that family.
No one would ever be envious of us, never say,
Look at them. See the happiness drip from their faces.

No. It was the year the word "maybe" pivoted
like a turnstile in the middle of our fights
as we made room for what went wrong and when,

the year you decided staying was more of a risk
than leaving. The year you had no fight left in you.
What a soul-crushing year it was. God. It was

the sink or swim year. The year I realized
everything alive in the world survives by adapting.
It was the year you taught me to tread water.

FORSYTHIA

I'm tired of all this beauty—
forsythia blooming as if to apologize
for the long, hard winter.
Soon the kids will hide
behind the trees growing
along the fence line.
They will hide and I will seek them
through the thin flush of color,
skinny arms and legs
transformed by laughter
in the numb drum of spring.
Those yellow branches
wave to me, call me to child's play,
but something in me refuses
this ordinary magic, distrusting
the muscle memory of kindness
even as the wind knocks buds
to the ground, without grace,
in the inexact language of April.

A cough, a tickle,
a sudden rise and froth
at the back of your throat—
something unnamed
dragged you out of bed,
heavy-footed, into mine.
You curl into me,
all chatter and conjunctions,
little "c" into big "C"
in the loose alphabet
of mother and daughter. Your skin,
infused with shampoo and half-sleep
rests against my grain,
silent as a star, each dip
and swirl of your curls
searching for the right word,
the form of things, how night
wraps its body around day
and asks for nothing but this
small moment. What keeps us awake,
other than the clock's sweeping hand
moving like a slow-cresting wave,
is the sound of no sound, the sound
of drifting, of grieving, of not letting go,
of trying to find a name for this.

Bury your tears in the yard with everything else
you hope might grow. Let the green stalks rise
to meet the sharp edge of your pruning shears.
Peace is what you seek right now. Pay no attention
to the back-and-forth of the grackles in their noisy
he said/she said conversation. What do they know
about the stone in your heart? What do they know about
the open throats of tulips choked by rot underneath?

Inside, dinner is on the table as the afternoon
drifts into dusk. Your family awaits your return.
Let them wait. Let your soft animal self breathe.
Now, take the shears and clip forsythia branches
for the dining room table. Make the room
dumb with beauty—let no one be the wiser.

Home Depot makes me weep.
I travel down aisles like a tourist
in the kingdom of tools
as I look for an extension cord,
a rake, lawn bags—
things you took with you
when you left for good.
I push the metal cart,
quiet as a carriage,
along the hardest of cement floors,
so unforgiving it makes my back ache.
Look at all that needs replacing:
wrenches, screws, a drill.
I reach for caulk to rim the bathtub,
a fluorescent light to replace
the burned-out halo
that flickers above my head
as I move about the kitchen.
There is no permanence
in these objects,
but a sort of emptiness
from what remains.
How unfair
to be in this big-box store
with its sky-high shelves,
and rows and rows of normal.

THE BLOWER OF LEAVES

Always there is sky after sky waiting to fall.
A million brilliant ambers twisting into

the thinning October sun, flooding my eyes
in a curtain of color. My yard is their landing strip.

Today I bow to the power of negative space,
the beauty of what's missing—the hard work

of yard work made harder without you,
while the stiff kiss of acorns puckers the ground.

I am a fool. Even as the red impatiens wither and brown,
they are still lovely. I feed the gaping mouths of lawn bags

with their remains. All this time I was waiting
for a heavy bough high above to crush us,

but really I was waiting for you to say *enough*.
It was a feeling that swirled inside me,

a dark congruence, a tempest of the blood pulsing *enough,
enough*. How I had mistaken it for ordinary happiness.

I can forgive the wind rustling the aging oaks,
the clusters of leaf mush trapped along the fence line,

but with you there is no forgiveness.
Only refuse. Only the lawn's dying clover

and weeds masquerading as grass.
Nothing is ever easy or true,

except the leaves. They all fall.
Dependable as a season.

1

Just along Salem Sound
south of Cape Ann
lies Great Misery—
83 acres of stone coast,
a tangle of worn trails
and grassy fields. You can
walk around its circumference
in a few hours and always
find your way back.

While four acres
of steep-sided shore
and unforgiving terrain
outline Little Misery.
Every curve
bends the fabric
of time
with its rugged
beauty.

Two islands,
one shadowing
the other,
both untouched
for years.

2

When asked if I saw it coming,
the leaving, I say, *No.*
I say,

When he slept
I put my hand on his chest,
felt his tremors, the rustle of sea grass.
I thought it nothing more than breathing
through uncomfortable sleep.

3

What was it like, when the 20s roared,
when vacationers docked their boats just off shore?
Summer retreats and gala parties,
a swell time at the clubhouse
encircled by towering aspens,
a respite for Bostonians
and townies with money
to burn.

Imagine a pier, a club house,
a swimming pool filled with salt water,
guest cottages to the horizon line,
a tennis court and tournaments,
a nine-hole golf course with caddies
dressed in pressed white linens.

So elegant, so glamorous a setting,
you can almost see a couple
looking out over a balcony,
hands entwined, the moon
hanging over them
by the thin thread of midnight.

4

I loved. You loved. We loved
with our whole selves—
lips first, then the tumble of skin

pulling each other down,
caught in the tangle and swirl,
closer to terror, closer to ourselves
the way we became something else
as soon as we were in it,
the way our bodies displaced truth
through the depths of anger,
the way it changed us
and we were changed by it.
We were poor swimmers
too far in the rip to be saved.

5

Four acres of wild beauty,
Little Misery,
reachable by wading
from its mate
across a shallow channel.

To be here is to feel
the relentless wind
gusting at all times.
None of the sheltering coves
of Great Misery
offer protection.
The easterly breeze
will gut a confession out of
the best of liars.

6

We were never of one body.
You said wind. I said water.
And whatever connected us has all but disappeared.

I was the reedy weeds clinging to the bottom edge of everything.
I was the red algae rotting on the shore in the summer heat.
I was the stinging salty air, the air around your tongue.

Out of your tongue you carved a boat.
Out of the boat you sailed to a new life.
Out of your lifeboat I was wrecked.
No man is an island but it lives inside of you,
adrift in you like a rupture, a fault,
magma rising from your ocean floor
as you become whoever you are becoming.

7

Mis·ery: noun. A state of suffering that results in poverty or
want; a circumstance, a thing, or a place inside that causes
discomfort or heartbreak; a state of great unhappiness or
emotional distress; a pain; a wretchedness; a grief; a woe.

8

Eighth anniversary,
I take off my two rings from my left hand,
place them side by side so they touch
to create the number eight.
So beautiful the alchemy.
Their gold patinas worn dull,
scratched and dented,
seemingly resilient, tested, loved
like the promise they enclose.
Two islands floating in choppy waters.
I turn them on their sides:
eight, infinity, forever.
Sun and moon, earth and sky,
husband and wife.

I place the rings in my nightstand drawer
and shut it hard. The last note
at the end of a song.

9

At low tide
I can see the cracked ribs
of a wrecked steamship
jutting above the waterline.

10

I love the kayak.
I love to set the long narrow pod,
slender as sea grass, into the water,
stir its pulse with the paddles
below the water's surface
while a briny mist sprays my face.
There is a silence here. It is simple
and flat and murky. I lean forward,
Go farther. Go deeper, I tell myself.
I came here for proof. Was it ever real?
I want to run my hand along
ruined structures and rotted wood,
cottages gutted by fire and never rebuilt.
I want to know the animals that have burrowed deep,
fed their young, killed their enemies,
survived the snow and ice another year
and for what?

My foolishness will tip me over—this, I know.
Can I paddle my way out of this?
With the turn of the shoulders,
I feel the dull rip of movement,
the hover and glide toward Misery.

Things happen, I tell myself.
People betray each other all the time.
Why did I think it otherwise?

11

Uncertainty keeps me wading.
I step on shells broken
long before we were born.
Give me mussels
entwined in seaweed,
dark and tightly curled
like my daughter's hair.
Give me red algae,
the disarticulated shells
of horseshoe crabs
abandoned for ruin,
with barnacles
attached to everything.

What remains is bankrupt:
stone and wood and sand and rot.
Maybe we expect too much from islands.

Sky
reflecting water
reflecting sky.
I wait for the sea
to take back memory.
My body shimmers back
at me under the hot July sun
revealing a body at rest.
I uncuff my jeans,
let the caked sand fall
over my painted toes,
listen to the water splash

and lap as it tells me
what it means to be patient—

how to endure erasure
and fill an empty space
with something more than
the subtraction of light.

The trick is to know where you're going
before you begin. Wet your hands.

Feel the floor with the soles of your feet
as you move the hard clay toward

the body. Your hands are the guide.
Here, there is no air—you must wedge

the clay to rid it of what remains,
always moving toward the center.

Feel yourself glide around the outside
of the surface spinning with the wheel

because speed and pressure will cause it to open.
You know this. Here, you can raise walls

with just your fingers. Hold it with a little give,
allow yourself this moment before the making begins.

TETHER

After stepping into the world again,
there is that question of how to love,
how to bundle yourself against the frosted morning—
the crunch of icy grass underfoot, the scrape
of cold wipers along the windshield—
and convert time into distance.

What song to sing down an empty road
as you begin your morning commute?
And is there enough in you to see, really see,
the three wild turkeys crossing the street
with their featherless heads and stilt-like legs
in search of a morning meal? Nothing to do
but hunker down, wait for them to safely cross.

As they amble away, you wonder if they want
to be startled back into this world. Maybe you do, too,
waiting for all this to give way to love itself,
to look into the eyes of another and feel something—
the pleasure of a new lover in the unbroken night,
your wings folded around him, on the other side
of this ragged January, as if a long sleep has ended.

JANUS, THE GOD OF BEGINNINGS AND ENDINGS, BUYS A NEW FRONT DOOR

Closed, it contained all our sadnesses,
when the "do us part" part of our marriage
came sooner than death yet felt like it anyway.

Hollow, wooden, with three diagonal windows at the top
it refused to let in light, even on the sunniest of days
when the stories belonged to the house,

stories of the previous owners
before the husband died of heart failure
and the wife was committed for dementia,

whispered about as the crazy lady
who chased neighborhood kids with a switch
and fed raw meat to squirrels and raccoons

from the front porch in a white slip.
Those stories were never ours;
we were wrong to keep them.

So when you left us unhinged
we ripped the door off the frame
and wood chips fell like confetti,

our natural history—now artifact.
We made our home into a dwelling of air,
where the miracle of light illuminates

every last speck of dirt and dead skin,
a place where misery and company can, for once,
show themselves the door:

a bright white entrance with an arch
of faux stained glass down the center
as a few stray rays bend and crinkle

across the kids' overnight bags, parked and waiting for you
next to the last of your belongings piled in a heap,
ready for donation or trash.

And Janus, already loud in the house of herself,
shows her children that loneliness can be
a kind of light, an opening

to the soft knocking of old hurts
where their own exquisite sides of the story
float like dust, waiting to be told.

because daylight won't save you
because a child's cry reverberates across
the deepest caverns of your heart, which is
dark and stained with old, rotted love,
yet you've given what's left of it to them.
How can you not get up, fix breakfast,
take out trash, pack lunches, brush teeth, wash faces,
kiss the tops of their heads as they hug you goodbye
with a long, firm squeeze that says, *Please come back.*
So there you sit in traffic like a slug on a highway
thinking *we're fucked.*
But you do it. You do it
because there's no one else, not any more.
Even in this starless time, soaked in the syllables
of questions without answers, more separation
than agreement, more null than void,
despite that mocking voice in your head, yours or his
—you just can't tell anymore—which says
you've been given these silver linings
who call you mommy.
Get up.

CUNT

—for SWS

It rolls off the tongue like a bullet train,
and once it leaves the station
that train is never late. You take it out
when your college-educated self
needs to tell it like it is. There's not
another word in the English language
to describe the moment your daughter,
your love child, comes back after a weekend
with your ex-husband and his new girlfriend,
the one he left you for when he said
he wanted to lead a more "authentic life."
You've spent your days not reacting
in front of the kids, for the sake of the kids—
but not this time. After 52 weeks of pickups
and drop offs, your turnstile of a mouth
swings open like a car door unhinged,
the moment your daughter tells you of her weekend,
you ask, *Why does your hair look so different?*
And she says, *Daddy's girlfriend combed it.*
She looks at you with those inquisitive brown eyes
half-knowing she's tripped the wire
between the said and unsaid.
You pull her into a hug, then send her into the kitchen,
dragging a deep breath out of the cave of yourself.
Regret is not in your vocabulary
because under your breath, barely audible,
you've just hurled the last word in the arsenal
you can draw back and launch like a punch in the face.

CLEAVER

Because not every woman
can afford a battle-axe,
or keep a scythe in the shed,
we know where the cleaver is kept,
our weapon of choice.
The square blade glistening
at the ready in the kitchen drawer
wrapped in the silence
of our best dish towel.
We bring it out during holiday meals
and Sunday dinners
when a knife just won't do.
Keepers of the kitchen,
protectors of the hearth,
how else would we cut through
a lifetime of meat and bone,
of sauces in need of garlic
smashed to smithereens
with the flat metal edge?
I have carved a turkey's carcass
as deftly as a butcher
on a Saturday afternoon.
But let's be practical, first cut,
deepest cut—not for the gentle or weak of will.
Who else can split an apple down the center
without disturbing the core?
Because, as in Zen tradition, we know
how to cleave the spaces in between bone
and never spill a drop of blood.

HOME IMPROVEMENT, PART 2

Friday nights are the best nights to meet men
at Home Depot. I travel down the aisles like a tourist
in the kingdom of tools looking for a weekend warrior,
someone a full score younger helping to re-stake
a friend's fence post, or building a rocking horse for his niece.
I need wrenches, screws, a drill—things taken when my ex
left for good.
                    Home Depot, home of the handy,
the amateur professional, and me with my *Hi,
can you help me?* look. Give me the guy
with the ratty college T-shirt, slim build, and galvanized grip,
a real DIY-er with the I-haven't-shaved-in-two-days grin.
Can you help me? I need hardware to mount
my flat screen. The smell of cedar is everywhere.
I'm fingering an edger in a wall full of edgers.
And what about spackle?
                    I need a sledgehammer.
Walls torn down and put back up. A fresh coat of paint
on new life. How unfair to be in this normal store
with its rows and rows of beautiful. I need a satin finish.

Alone in the basement,
I take off my pajama bottoms
and slide warm denim
from the dryer over my thighs.
They unfurl like a blue flag
tighter than I remember,
hanging lower and snugger
around my hips than before.
This is how 42 feels: authentic,
comfortable, dangerously curvy,
a little distressed along the pockets.
I run my hands over the weft and weave
smooth the creases over the inseam,
that junction between the invisible and visible
at the intersection of the crotch.
The long cursive of my legs
is my signature. Blessed be
the soap and hard water
that makes it all come clean.
Like fallen halos,
white rings of snow salt
once around my cuffs
tumbled away in turbulence,
my past sins absolved.
Everything smells April fresh,
of mountain breezes and waterfalls.
My body retrofits to these grooves and furrows,
and the selvage that never fades.

CHOCOLATE CHIP PANCAKES, 7 P.M.

Tonight, we do dinner easy.
I take measuring bowls
from the cabinets,

mix Bisquick, egg, and milk
with a wooden spoon,
fold the batter

while semi-sweets
drop from my daughter's fingers.
My son mans the griddle.

I hold his hand
as he flips with a spatula. Each cake
a toasted sun in a cast-iron sky.

Everything floats in a sea of syrup
in this unhurried hour
at the end of the day.

And my heart, full from laughter,
requires no napkin.
I lick happiness from my fingers.

From the crib, she bleats my name
like a wounded sheep, *Mama, Mama,*
in her soft whimpers. She says,
pa-pa broken, meaning pacifier.
She is too old for this kind of tether,
the constant sucking. In every photo,
it looks as if her smile has been plugged,
as if her teeth are growing around it,
so I snipped the tip, no suction, little comfort.
Eventually my daughter will not want it
or need it or need me. She is becoming
a soul in this world, always craving something.
And I, the person that she trusts more than anyone,
am the source of her distress. Tonight I silently
mourn this loss as I lean over the railing,
look into her watery brown eyes and tell her,
Yes, pa-pa's broken.

I tell my son
that the best poems
are written in the sand
and washed away with the tide.
I say the moon controls the waves,
uses the wind to rake the shore.
It is an open invitation to fill
the world with words
because like seashells
you can never have too many.
I tell him to wade into the water.
Start a conversation with
the tiniest grain on the beach,
the one that catches his eye with its glint.
It will tell him everything he needs to know
about this moment, about how to stay in it
a little longer. It will tell him how to be,
for an instant, the thing he most wants
to become.

ADVICE FOR MY SON UPON ENTERING KINDERGARTEN

Don't be surprised
if the other kids
wonder what you are.
They may make fun of your
new used backpack,
your brown-bag lunch.
They don't know
it's impolite to ask,
Where's your mama?
even when I'm standing
next to you, cautious as a nanny.
You are fair and smooth.
The girls will fall in love
with your long lashes,
while the boys will envy
the ease with which
you pass through worlds.
Be smart.
These boys may push,
cut you in line,
think they're entitled
to something more.
The playground
is an unlikely (or maybe
the most likely) place
to contemplate
the human condition.
They may look into
your coal-black eyes
and demand you
choose your color,
yet we know black or white
is not that simple.

You are the best of both.
It's your choice to choose
or not to. I say,
let that be your first
fuck you to the world.

—for my son

You are not who they say you are.
You are Nubian with white stripes

and sport a Mohawk for a mane.
Once hunted to extinction,

your deafening bray is a song for the fallen.
Some might even say you are God's mistake.

But how ordinary the world would be without you.
They will say stay in your herd, stick close to your mother's
    side.

Remember, you are all equine.
Put another way, you are a wild ass.

Raise those ears. Kick your legs.
Gaze that impenetrable stare.

Your forefathers once grazed on African grasses.
Your place in this world is the one you claim.

STRING THEORY

A baseball contains 330 yards of yarn coiled
inside its body. My son has at least that many nerves,

if not more, all pointed toward home plate.
I watch him prep for T-ball practice with

as much concentration as a six-year-old can muster.
When he throws, the ball never knows where it's going.

Let's not talk of velocity, the placement of thumb
and middle finger along tight, red stitches.

Save talk of revolutions for another day.
Throw the ball, catch the ball—that's it.

And a wild pitch gives way to unexpected joy
as the ball corkscrews and rolls near my feet,

a gift from the little-boy hand gripping these
covered strands of wool, hope released,

as he cocks his cap and lets another fly,
not caring at all where it lands.

I lather a dime of shampoo
in swift revolutions around your head—
your hair, a mess of rotini
bundled between my soapy hands.
I marvel at your dark curls—perfect,
especially the ones hiding
at the neck's nape,
softer than light and water
and always turning away.

Never will your hair be
the difficult straw of your mother's—
brittle and in need of relaxing.
Like a cyclone, your tresses
cannot be trained.
I pull a foam-covered strand,
let the tight helix wrap around
my finger; I get lost
in your rotation.

PRAYER

Tonight I pray to the god

of small children and broken toys.

Since it seems as though we are made

in Her image, thank you for the tiny curls

in my daughter's hair. Blessed is She

who holds those galactic swirls close to her beautiful head,

thanks for letting me run my fingers through them

as we read *Goodnight Moon* at the end of a long, wrecked day.

Thanks for her little hands with chipped nail polish

and the laughter ebbing from her coral lips.

God of the color pink, god of Dora the Explorer,

thank you for rain as we begin our journey into sleep,

let the sky fall one drop at a time.

That we can find ourselves

in this unearned sweetness,

to the god of small miracles

I say, *Amen*.

WHAT MY KIDS WILL WRITE ABOUT ME IN THEIR FUTURE TELL-ALL BOOK

They will say that no was my favorite word,
more than stop, or eat, or love.

That some mornings, I'd rather stay in bed,
laptop on lap, instead of making breakfast,
that I'd rather write than speak.

They will say they have seen me naked.
Front side, back side—none of which
were my good side.

They will say I breastfed too long.

In the tell-all book my kids will write
they'll tell how I let them wrinkle like raisins
in the bathtub so I could watch Big Papi at the plate.

They'll talk about how I threw out their artwork,
the watercolors and turkey hands,
when I thought they weren't looking
and when I knew they were.

They'll say that my voice was a slow torture,
that my singing caused them permanent hearing loss.

In the tell-all book my kids will write
as surely as I am writing this, they will say
I cut them off mid-sentence just because I could.

They'll tell you how I got down on my knees,
growling my low, guttural disapproval,
how I grabbed their ears, pinched the backs of their arms,
yet they never quite knew who was sadder for it.

They'll quote me saying, *I cry in the shower—*
it's the only safe place I can go.
They will say she was "our sweetest disaster."

They will say I loved them so much it hurt.

NOTES

"November 4, 2008": On this date, Barack Obama was elected the 44th president of the United States.

"Vivarium": The line "The night is long and slippery" is borrowed from Lynn Emanuel's poem "Homage to George Herriman," which appears in her collection *Noose and Hook*.

"Misery Islands": The islands Great Misery and Little Misery were named by shipbuilder Captain Robert Moulton, whose journal describes the three miserable days he spent on one of the islands during a fierce winter storm. In stanza 11, the line "Maybe we expect too much from islands" was inspired by a line in Dawn Paul's poem "Barnegat Island": "We expect a lot from islands."

"Janus, the God of Beginnings and Endings, Buys a New Front Door": The line "already loud in the house of herself" is borrowed from Anne Sexton's poem "The Double Image," which appears in her collection *To Bedlam and Part Way Back*.

"You Get Up": This poem was inspired by Ellen Doré Watson's poem of the same name, which appears in her collection *The Sharpening*.

ACKNOWLEDGMENTS

A number of poems first appeared in the following publications or websites. Many thanks to them all.

Academy of American poets, Poem-a-Day: "How to Love"
Connotation Press: "By Way Of," "You Are Not Your Salary"
Crab Creek Review: "Tether"
Fire on Her Tongue: "Body Politic," "In the Company of Women," "The Little Mermaid Walks Away," "Prayer"
Ibbetson Street #28: "Chocolate"
Ibbetson Street #31: "Bathing My Mother"
Journal of the Mothering Initiative: "Advice for My Son upon Entering Kindergarten," "Chocolate Chip Pancakes, 7 P.M.," "A Mother's Tale," "Never Let Them See You Cry," "Questions of Sleep," "Shampoo," "Treading Water" (as "The Year in Review"), "What My Kids Will Write in Their Tell-All Book," "You Get Up," "Zebra"
MiPoeisas: "Sleepover," "Vivarium"
Mom Egg Review: "What the Body Knows"
North American Review: "Conversion Theory," "January Is a Month You Would Consider Leaving"
Patch: "Demin"
Ploughshares: "The Blower of Leaves"

Soul-Lit: "After Making Love, I Leave to Write a Poem," "40," "Skinny Dip"

Ibbetson Street nominated "Chocolate" for a 2011 Pushcart Prize. *MiPoeisas* nominated "Sleepover" for a 2013 Pushcart Prize

With love and admiration to my poetry peeps: Joseph O. Legaspi, Colleen Michaels, Jennifer Jean, J. D. Scrimgeour, Kevin Carey, Dawn Paul, Cindy Veach Lappetito, Baron Wormser, Erin Dionne, Melissa Jolly, Eric Stich, Afaa Michael Weaver, Martha Collins, Major Jackson, Kathi Morrison-Taylor, Michael Ansara and Mass Poetry, and the Barbara Deming Memorial Fund. Gratitude to Nikky Finney, who gave me the right advice at the right time. And to the community of poets and writers in the blogosphere. In the words of the late, great Michael Jackson, "You rock my world."

Special thanks to my parents, family, and friends, near and far, always close to my heart.

CAVANKERRY'S MISSION

CavanKerry Press is committed to expanding the reach of poetry to a general readership by publishing poets whose works explore the emotional and psychological landscapes of everyday life.

OTHER BOOKS IN THE EMERGING VOICES SERIES